wise

happiness

meditations for life's journey

© Scripture Union 2007

First published 2007

ISBN 978 1 84427 310 2

207–209 Queensway, Bletchley, Milton Keynes, MK2 2EB, UK
www.wisetraveller.org.uk

All rights reserved. No part of this publication may be reproduced, stored in a retrieval system, or transmitted, in any form or by any means, electronic, photocopy, recording or otherwise, without the prior permission of the publisher.

Efforts have been made where appropriate and possible to secure permission to reproduce quoted material from copyright holders (see acknowledgements), but we apologise in the event of any oversights or omissions in this regard.

British Library Cataloguing-in-Publication Data: a catalogue record of this book is available from the British Library.

Cover image and text illustrations by Andrew Gray © 2007

The *Wise Traveller* logo (created by Andrew Gray)
© Scripture Union 2007

Andrew Gray has asserted his right under the Copyright, Designs and Patents Act 1988, to be identified as the illustrator of this work.

Cover and internal design and layout by x1.ltd.uk

Printed and bound by Henry Ling Ltd, Dorchester, England

Contents

Introduction 5

Adventurer 10
Blesser 14
Sensitiser 18
Dreamer 22
Giver 26
Pursuer 30
Builder 34
Unsettler 38
Reality-checker 42
Sufferer 46
Overcomer 50
Seer 54
Accepter 58
Kneeler 62
Thanks-giver 66
Joy-bringer 70

Background notes 74
Acknowledgements 78

Introduction

Many of us want a more spiritually satisfying life. This book is about catching hold of those moments of divine intensity that come our way in the midst of everyday living. As David Adam, a writer who draws on the inspiration of the ancient Celts, puts it, 'We need to walk with awe and wonder, we need to be aware of the deep mystery and power that flows through all things. … We need to discover again that there is an adventure to be lived in our world, a personal discovery to be made of the presence and the life that dances in all things.' And so this book is also about celebrating life as a journey, one which we 'walk with awe and wonder', recognising that there is something about the travelling, as well as the arriving, that should be treasured.

It's not always a popular theme, but by way of contrast to the hedonism of modern life is the view that worthwhile things take time, that process is important, and that taking the long way round cultivates traditional benefits such as patience and perseverance. This is what the journey can do for us. As we walk in solitude or in company we discover the power of the journey to prepare us, resource us and change us in ways that enhance our appreciation of the significant 'arrival' moments in our lives. Sure, it might be easier to drive straight to the packaged tourist experience, but the journey via the coastal path will have many compensations: the changing light on the ocean; the colour and contours of the cliffs; the seabird colonies perched precariously; the white sand draped like a scarf around the bay.

The *Wise Traveller* series offers wisdom for the journey; wisdom drawn from the spiritual classics of the Christian tradition alongside original reflections – stories, poems and meditations – that engage with the spiritual, emotional and, sometimes, brutal realities of life. As Proverbs 24:3,4 (TNIV) says: 'By wisdom a house is built, and through understanding it is established; through knowledge its rooms are filled with rare and beautiful treasures.'

This book has been written and compiled by people who would identify themselves as Christian in the broadest understanding of that term. These are people who have wrestled with what it means to live fully and who, time and time again, have turned to the Bible to find the wisdom, inspiration and guidance they need to carry on. At the back of the book you'll find notes that offer suggestions for further reading, showing where ideas and themes explored in the book originate in these ancient biblical writings that the Christian tradition has always recognised as sacred and God-inspired.

For many of us, seeking deeper fulfilment in life means increasing our sense of peace. This book offers opportunities to nurture stillness through contemplation. As you read, you may find it helpful to pause and reflect on your thoughts and feelings using the 'litany' or devotional pattern provided, a line of which appears on the first page of each chapter, accompanied by a woodblock-style illustration for those of us who find art a stimulus to meditation. The litany is inspired by the famous Celtic prayer, 'St Patrick's Breastplate', whose author, understanding Jesus to be the Son of God, calls upon him to be his companion and friend on each step of the journey:

Christ be with me, Christ within me,
Christ behind me, Christ before me,
Christ beside me, Christ to win me,
Christ to comfort and restore me.
Christ beneath me, Christ above me,

Christ in quiet, Christ in danger,
Christ in hearts of all that love me,
Christ in mouth of friend and stranger.

Whatever your spiritual convictions and hopes, I hope this collection blesses you on life's journey.

Phil Andrews
Series Editor

Other titles available
in the *Wise Traveller* series:

Loss

Relationships

Yet to be published:

Forgiveness

Growing

Hope

Adventurer

I see the path ahead of me...

When I plan adventures I've always been drawn North – over the seas and far away. Recently I spent some time in Helsinki, the farthest North I've ever been. The winter midday temperatures are regularly -20 °C and the roads and pavements are ice rinks. Drivers have to skid, pulling away from stops and taking corners with finely controlled wheel spins. Chaos and control are delicately balanced.

My natural inclination is that my future happiness depends on me being tightly in control of important choices, but often I get that wrong. I overestimate the effect that good and bad events will have on my happiness. Real adventures, the ones infused with a deeper happiness, demand a willingness to let go and trust.

There are stories of Celtic monks putting their trust in the divine. Imagine getting into a coracle and trusting that God would bring you to a safe harbour. That is an extreme example, but it illustrates for me the exciting possibility that there is a plan for me if only I would ease up a little on the steering wheel and try to find out what it is.

Bruce Stanley

It's tempting, Lord,
to stay at home
when faced with hard decisions.
To turn my back,
stay rooted in the soil of what I know
rather than look uncertainty right in the face,
although I think uncertainty has many faces
– or none – I'm not quite sure.

The world out there can seem so threatening,
the changes rapid, unexpected.
A frightened fledgling,
I'd rather nest in what I know,
than risk my wings in flight.
The nest is warm and undemanding
but its safety is unreal
and soon outgrown,
security as insubstantial

as the air I'm frightened of.
And staying at home
would breed a poverty of spirit
more dangerous than the journey.
Help me to find the courage, Lord,
to launch out into space
wherever you may lead.
To widen my horizons,
soar with confidence,
explore the possibilities
of life and love with you.
Take to the air on wings of faith
and fly.

Eddie Askew

Blesser

I see the road behind me...

Happy those at the bus stop in the rain, for they are on the route to heaven.

Happy those who hug the unhappy, for their hugs are a special currency.

Happy the schoolchildren dancing in puddles, for their splashes delight the aged.

Happy the fast-food avoiders, for they will be filled.

Happy the generous drivers, for they will enjoy satisfying journeys.

Happy the street buskers and *Big Issue* sellers, for their sight is true.

Happy the righteous banner-wavers and hippy nuclear-ship hammerers, for their innocence will be rewarded.

Happy those who stop the school yard fight, for the secret of life is theirs.

Happy the despised and ridiculed outsider, for they shall be home free.

John Davies

Each of us lives in two realms, the internal and the external. The internal is that realm of spiritual ends expressed in art, literature, morals, and religion. The external is that complex of devices, techniques, mechanisms, and instrumentalities by means of which we live. These include the house we live in, the car we drive, the clothes we wear, the economic sources we acquire — the material stuff we must have to exist.

There is always the danger that we will permit the means by which we live to replace the ends for which we live, the internal to become lost in the external. ...

This does not mean that the external in our lives is not important. We have both a privilege and a duty to seek the basic material necessities of life. Only an irrelevant religion fails to be concerned about man's economic well-being.

Religion at its best realizes that the soul is crushed as long as the body is tortured with hunger pangs and harrowed with the need for shelter. Jesus realized that we need food, clothing, shelter, and economic security. He said in clear and concise terms: 'Your Father knoweth what things ye have need of.'

But Jesus knew that man was more than a dog to be satisfied with a few economic bones. He realized that the internal of a man's life is as significant as the external. So he added, 'Seek ye first the kingdom of God, and his righteousness; and all these things shall be added unto you.' …

Martin Luther King, Jr (1929-1968)

Sensitiser

I see the land around me...

The desert in Christian tradition has symbolized the setting in which the traveller, stripped of non-essentials, comes face to face with God. It means a stark spiritual landscape with few landmarks, not to be crossed safely except by the highway called the way of holiness … It stands for a place of pilgrimage and passage from captivity to freedom. It represents a place of spiritual combat, where the powers of evil are likely to be discovered, without and within. … For the purpose of a retreat is to dispel illusion, to set aside distraction, and to penetrate the crust of superficiality in personal existence, which can deaden sensitivity to the reality of God.

Properly understood, therefore, retreat is not an escape into unreality, but the very opposite. It is a time for facing the truth … Consequently, a period of struggle may be necessary before the retreatant can enter into the peace of God, and experience inner 'rest' in harmony with God's will. For fantasies are slow to let go of their prisoners.

John Townroe

Life sometimes feels like a slow death – a seeping drowning, weighing me down by increments until I gasp for breath within a whirlpool of deadlines and expectations. And we call this 'earning a living'! I want to be truly alive, not striving for some dream existence that always seems to loiter on an elusive horizon.

Once, on a train, I travelled with a monk. I wondered how he could live with so few possessions and so many rules; and yet I found him gloriously free – liberated to be himself, happy with himself, truly alive and free to give back to life the gifts it had given him, freely offering that spark of life to me.

When I was a child life seemed simple, pressures were few and the summers endless. There was ample time to play, to be, to wonder, to be alive in each moment. I am travelling back to my childhood now. Taking a journey into a limitless landscape of simple contentment.

As I walk the old familiar route to my private room I choose to let slip my worldly cares; today there will be no diary, no computer, TV or phone. Alone I will seek the truth in my own simplicity, touched by what I encountered on that other journey; in my own way to wear a monk's habit and find a peace I have not known before.

All is quiet, all is still. Here there is nothing and yet everything. 'In your cell you will discover all there is to know', the brother had told me. And here perhaps all is found: myself; the world; being itself uncovered; God himself… In the solitude we are together, truly alive.

Steve Hollinghurst

Dreamer

I see who travels with me...

Some ask the world
   and are diminished
in the receiving of it.
    You gave me

only this small pool
    that the more I drink
from, the more overflows
    me with sourceless light.

RS Thomas (1913-2000)

When I was young, the television always seemed full of stories of people who had made grand and amazing dreams come true. The man who had climbed Everest, the woman who had revolutionised nursing, the people who had abolished slavery. These people inspired me, but they also made me unhappy at times, for I didn't feel I had the ability to realise ambitions on the scale of my dreams.

But then, by chance, I discovered someone who had little dreams. Once again, I discovered her on television, and I was intrigued. She was called Thérèse Martin, and she was a French nun who died aged just 24. Her dreams were different; they were about doing the smallest things beautifully in love, simply because they were for God. She was inspired by Jesus of Nazareth who once told a story about people who hadn't realised that when they served each other, they were really serving a higher purpose.

Thérèse wrote a diary, and in it she talked about her little dreams and I saw that her ambitions were realisable. They were full of simple ambitions, like smiling and being extra-nice to the people who grated on her nerves!

Thérèse was refreshingly honest about the little difficulties she faced over simple things, like sharing her possessions. She also shared practical hints about the small ways in which she was able to help others; looking out for opportunities such as that presented by an elderly nun with arthritic hands who couldn't reach the bread at mealtimes. These were little acts of blessing, and yet they were achievable. Achievements that often went unnoticed yet which made the world a better place.

And now, although I occasionally still get distracted by big dreams, I notice the world right in front of me, and see that it is full of little, but important, things: chance encounters, tiny words, shy smiles, tangible needs. When I focus on responding to these little things, I'm filled with happiness as I see the world around me impacted in small, but wonderful ways.

Sue Wallace

Giver

I see the ground beneath me...

Jesus looked at his followers and said, 'Happy you people who are poor, because the kingdom of God belongs to you. Happy you people who are now hungry, because you will be satisfied. Happy you people who are now crying, because you will laugh with joy. People will hate you, shut you out, insult you and say you are evil, because you follow the Son of Man. But when they do, you will be happy. Be full of joy at that time, because you have a great reward waiting for you in heaven. Their ancestors did the same things to the prophets.

'But how terrible it will be for you who are rich, because you will have had your easy life. How terrible it will be for you who are full now, because you will be hungry. How terrible it will be for you who are laughing now, because you will be sad and cry. How terrible when everyone only says only good things about you, because their ancestors said the same things about the false prophets.'

Luke 6:20–26 (The Bible, New Century Version)

Happiness is given. My happiest moment this week came late on Saturday afternoon when, on the edge of my seat at the football ground, I saw the ball fly into the roof of the opponents' net, for the second time in a minute, and impending defeat turned into dramatic victory. The happiness that sport can bring is often fleeting, so it's essential to savour it while it lasts.

Happiness is given. It's not earned, it's not bought, it's *given* to us. I didn't create the happiness I felt on Saturday. It came to me through a footballer's skill. On a deeper level, friendship, love — these things bring happiness because of the way others act and feel towards us, what they give to us.

When we're good at something, so often we call it a *gift*, or other people will say we're *gifted*. That is at the root of our happiness about our good work. Many people talk about the gift of a newborn baby; many people precede breakfast by consciously rejoicing in the gift of a new day.

If you believe happiness is given, then you can believe in the possibility of being surprised. Gifts surprise us. And if you believe happiness is given, then you can believe in the possibility that something new will come. There's always a chance that sometime, possibly when you least expect it, something new will bring a change.

The events of recent history bear this out. No one predicted that in 1989 people from East and West Berlin would be happily pulling the wall down together; no one foresaw that in the nineties South African blacks would be happily queuing to cast the first votes in their history.

Happiness is surprising; happiness is on its way – because happiness is given. So much in life can be taken as a gift, if our hearts and minds are tuned in to the giver.

John Davies

Pursuer

I see the sky above me...

Abba Macarius while he was in Egypt discovered a man who owned a beast of burden engaged in plundering Macarius' goods.

So he came up to the thief as if he was a stranger and helped him to load the animal.

He saw him off in great peace of soul saying, 'We have brought nothing into this world, and we cannot take anything out of this world, the Lord gave and the Lord has taken away; blessed be the name of the Lord'.

Macarius the Great (c300-390)

The US constitution expresses its understanding of 'happiness' in the phrase 'life, liberty and the pursuit of happiness'. Happiness is something we ought to have, something we have a 'right to pursue'. Our society is geared towards encouraging us to 'pursue' things. The pursuit of happiness slots in nicely with the pursuit of success, wealth, possessions, relationships, experiences, and this pursuit fuels the demand for ever more products and services to keep the capitalist engine running.

The advertisers understand that the pursuit of happiness is really the ultimate goal of the avid pursuer of commodities — that happiness is found with that car, or the set of friends that go with this drink, or the glamorous man or woman who offers those chocolates or this exotic holiday. Indeed the gurus of advertising realised long ago that you don't sell products in advertisements, you sell dreams and tell people that the dream comes with the product; you sell happiness to a culture that has been given the 'right' to pursue it.

In such a world my pursuit of happiness comes at a price. The goods that grant happiness are in limited supply, so that pursuing happiness becomes the same as competing for happiness. If I have that car and am 'happy', you cannot have it and so cannot be happy. There are young people on our poorest estates who come to know they will never have that car, so they steal it, exercising their 'right to pursue happiness'.

But how happy are those who are ahead in the pursuit of happiness? The truth is that happiness is denied them too; they are destined *always* to pursue happiness, as a changing array of goods ensures that attaining it becomes something that can never be achieved through purchase power.

What if we decided to stop pursuing happiness for ourselves and instead saw it as a gift to supply to others? Then happiness is a gift that having been received might just encourage another to do the same for someone else, who might do the same for another, who might do the same for... It just has to start with somebody giving generously with no thought of themselves...

Steve Hollinghurst

Builder

I see the path ahead of me...

The story is told of a man (in the pre-mechanization era) who, while walking down a country lane, came across a stone quarry in which a number of men were working. He questioned several of them about what they were doing. The first replied irritably, 'Can't you see? I'm hewing stone.' The second answered without looking up, 'I'm earning £100 a week.' But when the same question was put to the third man, he stopped, put his pick down, stood up, stuck out his chest and said, 'If you want to know what I'm doing, I'm building a cathedral.' So it is a matter of how far we can see. The first man could not see beyond his pick, and the second beyond his Friday pay packet. But the third man looked beyond his tools and his wages to the ultimate end he was serving. He was co-operating with the architect. However small his particular contribution, he was helping to construct a building for the worship of God.

John Stott

One day, when I was 7, my primary school teacher said the most bizarre thing, which, I think, is why I remembered it.

'You'll never see an unhappy nun,' she remarked. 'You might see an angry nun, or a busy nun, or a tired nun, but never an unhappy nun.' So, of course, I took that as a personal challenge. Every time I saw a nun, I'd look at her face to see if she was unhappy, and once I saw one crying, although it was at a funeral… Being a nun doesn't preserve you from normal human suffering then. What makes nuns distinctive is that they choose (or are chosen by) a radical lifestyle of service which they embrace with their whole being.

Maybe what my teacher really meant by her statement was that if you are doing the job you feel you are 'meant' to do, it brings its own sort of inner contentment, one that comes from knowing you are in the right place. For all of us, squeezing into someone else's shoes will only make our feet hurt.

Sue Wallace

God has created me to do Him some definite service;
He has committed some work to me
which He has not committed to another.
I have my mission – I may never know it in this life,
but I shall be told it in the next.
I am a link in a chain,
a bond of connection between persons.
He has not created me for naught,
I shall do good, I shall do His work. ...
Therefore, I will trust Him. Whatever, wherever I am.
I can never be thrown away.
If I am in sickness, my sickness may serve Him;
in perplexity, my perplexity may serve Him;
if I am in sorrow, my sorrow may serve Him.
He does nothing in vain. He knows what He is about.
He may take away my friends.
He may throw me among strangers.
He may make me feel desolate, make my spirits sink,
hide my future from me – still He knows what He is about.

John Henry Newman (1801-1890)

Unsettler

I see the road behind me...

By entering through faith into what God has always wanted to do for us — set us right with him, make us fit for him — we have it all together with God because of our Master Jesus. And that's not all: We throw open our doors to God and discover at the same moment that he has already thrown open his door to us. We find ourselves standing where we always hoped we might stand — out in the wide open spaces of God's grace and glory, standing tall and shouting our praise.

There's more to come: We continue to shout our praise even when we're hemmed in with troubles, because we know how troubles can develop passionate patience in us, and how that patience in turn forges the tempered steel of virtue, keeping us alert for whatever God will do next. In alert expectancy such as this, we're never left feeling shortchanged. Quite the contrary — we can't round up enough containers to hold everything God generously pours into our lives through the Holy Spirit!

Romans 5:1-5 (The Bible, The Message version)

The tribe finally settled in a new land at the end of the summer, far away from where they had set out from months before. Scouts had been sent ahead to select the right location. None they passed through seemed perfect but with winter approaching a decision had to be made. That first winter was difficult for every member of the tribe. Food was scarce and the reserves from the summer's hunting, that which could be carried, soon ran out.

In those first few years there was much to challenge them and much to learn. Migration routes of the local wildlife were discovered, providing a reliable source of meat; the best fishing sites were found through trial and error; the forests were scoured for any food above and below ground. Nothing in life was easy but the tribe was happy, absorbed and united in overcoming the trials of surviving.

With sources of sustainable food guaranteed, the tribe turned their attention to devising more time-saving and technologically refined ways of improving their existence. As the decade became two, the people grew increasingly comfortable as the challenges of their new territory faded. With this came the growth of boredom amongst the tribe; conflicts broke out more frequently and ill-health increased. A full generation on from their arrival at the new location the elders of the tribe, weighing up the situation, decided it was time to move again – as they, and their predecessors, had done the last time and the time before that.

The wisdom of these elders was to know when the time was right to change direction; to journey into unfamiliar territory. They recognised that their well-stocked and established home had become exhausted of treasure in ways more subtle, but just as threatening to their happiness, as if the land had been stripped bare and the rivers drained. What lay ahead out of sight around the corner would challenge them, but it would enrich them much more than standing still.

Bruce Stanley

Reality-checker

I see the land around me...

The singer-songwriter Elliott Smith said, '"Depressing" isn't a word I would use to describe my music. But there is some sadness in it – there has to be, so that the happiness in it will matter.'

Elliott Smith knew the rare value of happiness because he was among the 20 million North Americans diagnosed with clinical depression and the further 20 million suffering anxiety disorders. This proved fatal for him – at 34 he took his own life after an argument with his girlfriend.

Smith was never a star, but his music continues to be a focus for thousands of people who find that his songs of honest struggle faithfully express their own hard-won hopes. He belongs among those most respected artists who are best able to articulate the complex relationship between happiness and pain which all of us know.

Against the relentless torrent of success and celebrity, the truly compelling artists are those who strive so much with life that their happiness – when it comes – has great integrity.

John Davies

The characteristic of human nature is to love oneself and to consider only one's self. But what else can it do? It cannot help its own love being inconsistent and miserable. It wants to be great and sees that it is only small. It wants to be happy and finds it is wretched. It wants to be perfect and sees itself full of imperfections. It wants to be the object of other people's love and esteem and sees that its faults deserve only their dislike and contempt. Finding itself in this predicament, it reacts in the most unjust and criminal passion imaginable. For it conceives a deadly hatred of the truth that would rebuke it and convince it of its faults. It would like to eliminate this truth, and not being able to destroy it, it represses it as much as it can in the consciousness of itself and others. So it takes every precaution to hide its own faults from itself and from others, and cannot bear to have them pointed out or even noticed.

Unquestionably it is an evil to be so full of faults, but it is a still greater evil to be full of them and yet unwilling to acknowledge them, since this results in the further evil of deliberate self-delusion.

Blaise Pascal (1623–1662)

Sufferer

I see who travels with me...

I have a friend called Rachel, who suffers from severe enduring depression after being abused as a child. She's had a tough life, often being pushed around and patronised by others, or being shunted in and out of a variety of hospitals.

I asked her once, how she kept travelling with hope when the road around her seemed so bleak. She replied, 'For me, depression is when you wake up and someone has stripped the colours from the world, leaving it grey. I can feel desperately alone even if I am surrounded by people. Yet the thing that keeps me going is forcing myself to see and smell the flowers, to really comprehend the beauty of the world around. To know there is a God. It sounds simple. But it's not simple to me, I have to fight to do it, and that keeps me going. But it's not all bad. If this illness has taught me anything, it's taught me perseverance. It's taught me to hope. It's taught me tolerance and understanding of others.'

Sue Wallace

HELMSMAN Blest be the boat.

CREW God the Father bless her.

HELMSMAN Blest be the boat.

CREW God the Son bless her.

HELMSMAN Blest be the boat.

CREW God the Spirit bless her.

ALL God the Father,
God the Son,
God the Spirit,
Bless the boat.

HELMSMAN What can befall you
And God the Father with you?

CREW No harm can befall us.

HELMSMAN What can befall you
And God the Son with you?

CREW No harm can befall us.

HELMSMAN What can befall you
And God the Spirit with you?

CREW No harm can befall us.

ALL   God the Father,
God the Son,
God the Spirit,
With us eternally.

HELMSMAN   What can cause you anxiety
And the God of the elements over you?

CREW   No anxiety can be ours.

HELMSMAN   What can cause you anxiety
And the King of the elements over you?

CREW   No anxiety can be ours.

HELMSMAN   What can cause you anxiety
And the Spirit of the elements over you?

CREW   No anxiety can be ours.

ALL   The God of the elements,
The King of the elements,
The Spirit of the elements,
Close over us,
Ever eternally.

'Sea prayer',
Carmina Gadelica

Overcomer

I see the ground beneath me...

If I were you I wouldn't be happy, a life changed for ever by a random accident. A promising career cut short. If I were you I would be angry, bitter, depressed. I've met people like that and understand their feelings, but I don't understand your happiness. You even seem able to joke about it in ways no one else would dare. I've also seen the effort you expend on being positive and am sure that at times it must be a real struggle, but your laughter is genuine and comes from somewhere deep within. If I were you I think I'd complain, ask for compensation and 'special' treatment. You refuse all this, insisting you're simply 'differently-abled'. I find that hard to comprehend, but I guess you are far too alive to be called 'dis-abled'. If I were you I'd have given up long ago, but you keep going and in spite of everything are indeed happy; happy with yourself and so are able to bring joy to others. I wish I knew your secret, even though I'm not like you. Neither am I happy.

Steve Hollinghurst

In this world nobody can escape from some suffering and the Cross; it is necessary to pass through the valley of the shadow of death (Psalm 23:4) for a longer or shorter period. But true Christians who bear their Cross 'die', yet they 'live', and in the midst of persecution are like the leaves of a tree which fall in winter, only to appear in renewed vigour in the spring, and prove they are really living (2 Corinthians 4:8–10; 6:4–10). In spite of sorrow and suffering their life is hid in God. Like the Gulf Stream, which protects the northern lands from the severe cold by its warm currents of water flowing across the ocean, so the hidden stream of the love of God and the current of the Holy Spirit protect and keep His people joyful and content.

Sadhu Sundar Singh (1889-1929)

Happy are those whose
help is the God of Jacob,
whose hope is in the Lord their God,
who made heaven and earth,
the sea, and all that is in them;
who keeps faith forever;
who executes justice for the oppressed;
who gives food to the hungry.

The Lord sets the prisoners free;
the Lord opens the eyes of the blind.
The Lord lifts up those who are bowed down;
the Lord loves the righteous.
The Lord watches over the strangers;
he upholds the orphan and the widow,
but the way of the wicked he brings to ruin.

Psalm 146:5-9
(The Bible, New Revised Standard Version)

Seer

I see the sky above me...

This joy is not, like earthly happiness, at once felt by the heart; after gradually filling it to the brim, the delight overflows throughout all the mansions and faculties, until at last it reaches the body. Therefore, I say it arises from God and ends in ourselves, for whoever experiences it will find that the whole physical part of our nature shares in this delight and sweetness. While writing this I have been thinking that the verse *'Dilatasti cor meum,'* [Psalm 119:32] 'Thou hast dilated my heart,' declares that the heart is dilated. This joy does not appear to me to originate in the heart, but in some more interior part and, as it were, in the depths of our being.

St Teresa of Avila (1515-1582)

Happiness comes in so many guises: euphoria at a moment of achievement; the relief at the ending of a 'difficult' day; the feeling you get in the company of a good friend; the delight when your favourite tune comes on the radio. My feeling about it now is that true happiness is more like complete peace, a sense of contented belonging. In this peace, everything seems to 'belong'; everything seeming to share this moment with me. Or rather I'm sharing this moment with everything, as if I have stumbled across some act of devotion poured out by creation and have been graciously allowed to stay and become part of it. The sound of adoration varies: the cathedral choir's four-part Easter anthem, the ancient rhythm of monastic chant, the rousing sound of the Stretford End celebrating another goal. This praise is almost silent, a sort of hum of life melding together the chirping of crickets, the song of birds, the sound of bees content with honey; the rolling of water gently over stone; nature's evensong. Even the trees seem to celebrate with a show of autumn gold replayed in the hue of a bowing sun.

And he is there – the one who inspires the Easter praise, and fills the monk's devotion, the one who gives us talents, the one who is the very source of creation. This devotion is the echo of his life breathed in all things, inspiring all things, at one with all things. This moment is a privilege; complete happiness; happy completion. A privilege I wish could be shared by those who never feel peace: the lonely, the suffering, the frightened. A privilege we deny to so much of the world through our careless destruction. He is in there with the suffering too, arms outstretched, sharing the pain, embracing all creation, drawing it into himself – the Maker remaking, bringing his at-one-ment.

Steve Hollinghurst

Background Notes

Page 11: Throughout the Christian Scriptures people are depicted as journeying in faith, treading the sometimes uncomfortable path of replacing control with trust in God. The book of Hebrews (11:1, NLT) says: 'What is faith? It is the confident assurance that what we hope for is going to happen. It is the evidence of things we cannot yet see.' When spiritual communities are built on this kind of authentic faith (like that of the Celtic monks) they have a unique contribution to make to human happiness.

Page 15: These sayings are inspired by Jesus' teaching about the character of the kingdom of God in Matthew's Gospel (5:1–12). The kingdom is defined as a new order of peace and fullness of life that Jesus himself ushers in through his own life, death and resurrection. As these 'beatitudes' suggest, entering this kingdom will take a childlike dependence on him.

Pages 20,21: Monastic retreats are popular in our busy age, not just to get away but to focus on what really matters. Jesus said that he came to give abundant life (see John 10:10) to those who would take the trouble to follow him.

Pages 24,25: Thérèse of Lisieux's diary is entitled *The story of a soul* (*L'histoire d'une âme*, Tan Books, 1997). Matthew's Gospel recounts Jesus' story about God commending a group for feeding the hungry or visiting the sick and imprisoned: 'Truly I tell you, whatever you did for one of the least of these brothers and sisters of mine, you did for me' (Matthew 25:40, TNIV).

Pages 28,29: Each of the beatitudes in Matthew 5:3–11 contains a promise – an often surprising free gift of blessing for those who will receive it from a giver recognised as God. And

I have seen the sun break through
to illuminate a small field
for a while, and gone my way
and forgotten it. But that was the pearl
of great price, the one field that had
the treasure in it. I realise now
that I must give all that I have
to possess it. Life is not hurrying

on to a receding future, nor hankering after
an imagined past. It is the turning
aside like Moses to the miracle
of the lit bush, to a brightness
that seemed as transitory as your youth
once, but is the eternity that awaits you.

RS Thomas (1913-2000)

I once heard a story of a transforming moment in the life of a woman who had been searching for happiness and healing for years. It seems she'd had a resolutely negative impression of herself. Although she'd earnestly sought wholeness all she ever seemed to express was how difficult life was for her and confirm that she was a victim – as if that was the easiest place to stay. Her identity seemed to be rooted in being that way.

One evening, a twinkly and entertaining old man was the visiting speaker at an event in her community. He had a reputation for wise words and healing prayers. After he had spoken people would approach him for a personal consultation. When the unhappy woman went up and immediately started pouring out her woes to him, his face suddenly screwed up in frustration and he said to her, 'Just *stop* thinking about yourself!' She was taken aback as if she'd been slapped in the face! In her mind she tried to formulate some response along the lines of, 'But shouldn't you feel sorry for me?' The words almost reached her lips but then she looked at the old man's unwavering frown and stood silently, chewing over his words.

Perhaps his wisdom had been in knowing what was the right thing to say at the right time, because a moment later she was different. Her route to more meaningful happiness had been revealed.

This woman learned that whatever it is you think you are lacking to be happy – understanding, kindness, friendship, respect, love – you have to give it, create it, make it for other people. She had learned not to measure herself by what she lacked, all the things she hadn't got, but to see what happened when she worked with what she had got, because however little that seemed, it could grow.

Bruce Stanley

Accepter

I see the path ahead of me...

Lord Jesus, come with me into the darkness of the cellar where I have hidden so many frightening things. I've shoved feelings down there because there wasn't time to process them – memories I couldn't face, emotions I thought were wrong and must be suppressed, fears, doubts, resentment and yes, furious anger! Shine your light on these things I never wanted to see again, and help me remember things I would much rather forget. Handle my reactions with me, and show me how to bear the pain of it all. I am so afraid of the dark; please come with me, and one by one we can bring these things to the surface and out into your sunlight. Lord, I am ashamed that I felt as I did, and as I still do. Forgive me, heal me, help me to let it go. I give you my darkness, and in exchange I receive your light.

Jennifer Rees Larcombe

I used to be terrified of exams, especially practical exams. If I had to do physical activities, such as driving a car, with someone scrutinising my every move, it made me so self-conscious that I began to tremble. This is probably why I failed my second driving test – I couldn't use the clutch properly as my leg was shaking so much!

What helped me was remembering something that had taken place in the days before my first written exam at school, when I was worrying about the whole experience. My mother came up to me and said, 'You know I don't care whether you pass or fail, as long as you have tried. That's what matters. And I know that you really will try.'

She's still the same. When I failed my first driving test, she gave me a hug and opened a bottle of champagne anyway, despite my protests that she should save it until I did eventually pass my test. She said that I needed cheering up and that I deserved it for trying.

It was this level of acceptance that made it possible for me to eventually pass, and in the meantime to be happy, despite not experiencing the success I wanted. With this came self-acceptance. I wasn't burdened with the pressure of other people's expectations of what I should be able to do or paralysed by the fear of failure. Being accepted by someone else has helped me to accept myself and treat myself with greater kindness, not based on hitting targets, but on my own awareness that I had made an effort despite experiencing fear. It's released me to become the person I really can be.

Sue Wallace

Kneeler

I see the road behind me...

My heart is not proud, O LORD,
my eyes are not haughty;
I do not concern myself with great matters
or things too wonderful for me.
But I have stilled and quietened my soul;
like a weaned child with its mother,
like a weaned child is my soul within me.

O Israel, put your hope in the LORD
both now and for evermore.

Psalm 131 (The Bible, New International Version)

There's nothing remarkable about Mendips, John Lennon's childhood home, now a national tourist attraction. It's in Scouse suburbia, semi-detached Woolton with a view of the woods opposite, birds singing, vehicles thudding past between town and airport, or en route to well-to-do parts of Cheshire where some Woolton folk would aspire to be. Inner-city aspirants end up in this area. There's nothing shoddy about Mendips either. It's a nice place to live. Nice, but unremarkable.

'Did Lennon's surroundings inspire his art?', an interviewer asked Yoko Ono on the occasion of the public opening of the house. She may have wanted to say yes – which would justify her investment in the place – but her instinctive answer was, 'No, it came from inside him,' which is probably closer to the truth.

Closest to the truth about what nurtured Lennon's art is probably the way Aunt Mimi brought him up, in an unremarkable, firm but supportive way. In Mendips, Mimi nurtured happiness.

The house played its part, brutally, through formative experiences like twice seeing family members killed on that fast road outside – vehicles were fewer and slower in the fifties, but no less deadly. And gently, because it's the sort of place of light, space and calm which helps creative minds flourish.

The National Trust and Yoko put a lot of effort into conserving Mendips. Objectors who sneered at the project said, incorrectly, 'This isn't what the National Trust was set up to do.' But with hotel-leisure developers closing in on a purchase, Yoko made a commitment that the house would be kept as a 'shrine': 'Better a shrine than a ruin,' as she sagely put it.

The great thing about Mendips is that it isn't 'great' at all. The great thing about preserving it for the nation is that it serves as a tribute to ordinary, decent folk like Mimi, to households struck by everyday tragedy, warmed by companionship and love, and to bedroom dreamers like Lennon without whose wit, daft wisdom and guileless invention the nation might arguably be less 'great' than it is. Happiness is nurtured in such places. Happiness begins at home.

John Davies

Thanks-giver

I see the land around me...

O Joyful Light of the holy glory of the immortal, heavenly, holy blessed Father, O Jesus Christ. Having come to the setting of the sun, having beheld the evening light, we hymn the Father, Son, and Holy Spirit, God. Meet it is at all times to hymn Thee with reverend voices, O Son of God, Giver of Life, wherefore the whole world doth glorify Thee.

'Phos Hilaron', second-century Greek hymn

Giving thanks and expressing gratitude increases your happiness and hopefully the happiness of others. Finding things to be thankful for is to make the choice of interpreting the past in a certain light. It might not seem easy to start with, but the more you do it the more it'll become natural. Why not try out some of the exercises below:

- In a journal write a list of things for which you can be thankful for that day. The list can be in any detail you like and it is important to find the frequency, time and place that is right for you. For some people it works best before they go to bed, to set the day in order; others like to do it five times a week over lunch!

- Write a 'thank you' message or email to someone who has contributed to your happiness, perhaps someone who you neglected to thank before or have taken for granted. It might take you a bit of practice to be able to articulate the reason for your gratitude, especially if it was something they said or did years before, but it will have more of an impact on the person you are thanking if you can be specific. After you've sent the message, give them space to respond.

- Start or add ten things to a list of *everything* you can be thankful for. Eventually this might be a very, very long list.

- When with friends, try to find ways to share things you are all thankful for, instead of, or as well as, talking about your woes and struggles.

- Try to remember how many times you said 'thank you' in the last 24 hours and try and double it in the next 24 hours.

- When you've received gratitude, kindness or a gift from others find a way to pass your happiness on to someone else. Let your happiness be all-pervasive, spreading throughout your life and overflowing into your relationships. Look out for changes in the way people respond to you and feel about themselves.

Bruce Stanley

Joy-bringer

I see who travels with me...

with each promise comes a happiness that runs deeper than the fleeting joy that comes from pleasure and success, and which can be discerned from time to time spilling out into world events where freedom and unity unexpectedly overcome tyranny.

Pages 32,33: We so often confuse happiness with wealth and possessions. Jesus tells us to store up spiritual treasure (see Matthew 6:19,20) and that to give away our life in his service is the key to truly finding it (see Matthew 10:39).

Page 36: Romans 12:6–8 outlines the range of gifts and vocations given to people in order to serve Jesus within the Christian community: 'We have different gifts, according to the grace given to each of us. If your gift … is serving, then serve; if it is teaching, then teach; if it is to encourage, then give encouragement … if it is to show mercy, do it cheerfully' (TNIV). Fulfilment comes with commitment to working out the calling God has given.

Pages 40,41: There are parallels between the experiences of the tribe and the way Jesus' inexperienced followers discovered how to live out what he had taught them. They found that it was as they faced challenges that they developed and matured, learning to trust in the resources that he had given them (see Luke 10:17). Later, the apostle James would write: 'Consider it pure joy, my brothers and sisters, whenever you face trials …' (see James 1:2–4, TNIV). He knew that we grow when placed outside of our comfort zones in ways that develop longer lasting emotional, psychological and spiritual capital than pleasure and ease bring.

Page 43: 'Blessed are the poor in spirit, for theirs is the kingdom of heaven … Blessed are the pure in heart, for they will see God' (Matthew 5:3,8, TNIV). Both these beatitudes of Jesus speak of the integrity of, and the promise for, those who struggle but endure in their commitment to him.

Page 47: Rachel's name has been changed and her story used with permission. She has been inspired by these words of the apostle Paul, whose hope and knowledge of God came through his following Jesus, and sustained him in his sufferings (many of which arose from his service of Jesus): '... and yet we live on; beaten, and yet not killed; sorrowful, yet always rejoicing; poor, yet making many rich; having nothing, and yet possessing everything' (2 Corinthians 6:9,10, TNIV).

Page 51: Those who are able to be happy in spite of the adversity they face show that happiness is about one's attitude to life not what happens to you. In the New Testament we see the difference that faith in Jesus made for his followers. Paul reveals that while he struggled with a severe affliction God spoke to him and said, 'My grace is enough; it's all you need. My strength comes into its own in your weakness' (2 Corinthians 12:8, *The Message*).

Pages 56,57: Jesus encouraged his followers into a radical way of life where giving was the first step and the first step was always ours to take: 'Give, and it will be given to you. A good measure, pressed down, shaken together and running over, will be poured into your lap. For with the measure you use, it will be measured to you' (Luke 6:38, TNIV).

Pages 60,61: Christian spirituality is often marked by a yearning for truly persevering, generous love, which is seen as God-given and personified in Jesus. It is this yearning that the apostle John articulates when he tells his followers, 'Whoever lives in love lives in God, and God in them' (1 John 4:16, TNIV). Such love stops our fear of failure and frees us to live with integrity, fulfilling our potential.

Pages 64,65: In Jesus' promise, 'Blessed are the meek, for they will inherit the earth' (Matthew 5:5, TNIV), meekness does not mean weakness. It speaks to those who are humbled in life and who are strengthened through acceptance and dependence upon God (see Romans 4:13). This promised inheritance relates to 'the renewal of all things' which Jesus refers to in Matthew 19:28, and the regenerated earth which Paul writes about in Romans 8:18–25. Life in Mendips encompassed a meekness which gave birth to extraordinary promise, testifying to the power of enlightened order and quiet acceptance.

Pages 68,69: Giving thanks to God is built into many Judeo-Christian rituals (see 1 Chronicles 16 and Matthew 15:36). Often we need to make a deliberate choice to focus on the edifying aspects of life, as we try to live generously and with integrity: 'Fix your thoughts on what is true and honourable and right. Think about things that are pure and lovely and admirable. Think about things that are excellent and worthy of praise' (Philippians 4:8, NLT).

Pages 72,73: According to the Christian Scriptures God was reconciling the world to himself in the life, death and resurrection of his Son (see 2 Corinthians 5:18). The atonement that Christ's death has brought into the world is the cure for all we have done, or not done, that has destroyed the quality of life we have as individuals and in relationship with each other, God and creation. It is identified as the source of harmony and reconciliation that will affect the whole of creation (see Revelation 21:1–5).

Acknowledgements

The Editor would like to thank the following for their help with the development of *Wise Traveller*: John Drane, Ray Simpson, Jonny Baker, Lizzie Green, Venetia Horton and, especially, Matt Campbell, whose contribution to the series is incalculable!

Original writing

Pages 11,40,41,56,57,68,69 © Bruce Stanley. Bruce is a creative project developer and life coach based in Bristol. www.embody.co.uk

Pages 15,28,29,43,64,65 © John Davies. John is an Evertonian with a high tolerance for suffering. He is also a vicar. www.johndavies.org

Pages 20,21,32,33,51,72,73 © Steve Hollinghurst. Steve lives in Manchester and works in Sheffield as a researcher. onearthasinheaven.blogspot.com

Pages 24,25,36,47,60,61 © Sue Wallace. Sue is music and arts co-ordinator for Visions in York. www.visions-york.org

Scripture Union takes no responsibility for the content of websites and blogs listed here that it does not directly operate. For further information about *Wise Traveller*: www.wisetraveller.org.uk.

Quotations

Research by Andrew Clark, Mark Laynesmith, Carsten Lorenz and Ellen Wakeham.

Page 5 David Adam, 'Listen', *Wisdom is calling*, edited by Geoffrey Duncan (Canterbury Press, 1999).

Pages 7,8 'St Patrick's Breastplate', translated by CF Alexander (1906).

Pages 12,13 Eddie Askew, *Unexpected Journeys* (The Leprosy Mission, 2002). Available from www.tlmtrading.com.

Pages 16,17 Martin Luther King, Jr, 'The man who was a fool', quoted in *Strength to Love* (Fount, 1987).

Page 19 John Townroe, 'Retreat', *The Study of Spirituality*, edited by Cheslyn Jones, Geoffrey Wainwright, Edward Yarnold (SPCK, 1986).

Page 23,55 RS Thomas, 'Gift', 'The Bright Field', *Collected Poems, 1945–1990* (JM Dent, a division of The Orion Publishing Group, 2000).

Page 27 Scriptures quoted from The Holy Bible, New Century Version (Anglicised Edition) copyright © 1993 by Nelson Word Ltd, 9 Holdom Ave, Bletchley, Milton Keynes, MK1 1QR.

Page 31 Macarius the Great, from *The Sayings of the Desert Fathers: The Alphabetical Collection*, translated by Benedicta Ward (Cistercian Publications, 1975).

Page 35 John Stott, *New Issues Facing Christians Today*, copyright © 1984, 1990, 1999, by John Stott. Used by permission of Zondervan.

Page 37 John Henry Cardinal Newman, *Meditations and Devotions, Part III: Meditations on Christian Doctrine* (1855). Used by permission of The Fathers of the Birmingham Oratory.

Page 39 Scripture taken from *THE MESSAGE* © 1993, 1994, 1995, 1996, 2000, 2001, 2002. Used by permission of NavPress Publishing Group.

Pages 44,45 Blaise Pascal, *The Mind on Fire*, edited by James M Houston (Hodder & Stoughton, 1991).

Pages 48,49 Alexander Carmichael, *Carmina Gadelica: Hymns and Incantations Collected in the Highlands and Islands of Scotland in the Last Century* (Lindisfarne Press, 1992).

Page 52 Sadhu Sundar Singh, *The Cross is Heaven: The Life and Writings of Sadhu Sundar Singh,* edited by AJ Appasamy (Lutterworth Press, 1956).

Page 53 Scripture quotations from the New Revised Standard Version Bible, copyright © 1989 by the Division of Christian Education of the National Council of the Churches of Christ in the USA, are used by permission. All rights reserved.

Page 59 Jennifer Rees Larcombe, *Turning Point: Is there hope for broken lives?* (Hodder & Stoughton, 2006).

Page 63 Scripture quotations taken from the HOLY BIBLE, NEW INTERNATIONAL VERSION. Copyright © 1973, 1978, 1984 by International Bible Society. Used by permission of Hodder & Stoughton Publishers, a member of the Hodder Headline Group. All rights reserved.

Page 67 Translation used by permission of the Russian Orthodox Church Outside of Russia.

Page 71 St Teresa of Avila, *The Interior Castle* or *The Mansions*, translated from the *Autograph of St Teresa of Jesus* by the Benedictines of Stanbrook (Thomas Baker, 1921).

Page 74,77 Scripture quotations are taken from the Holy Bible, New Living Translation, copyright © 1996. Used by permission of Tyndale House Publishers, Inc, Wheaton, Illinois 60189. All rights reserved.

Page 74–77 Scripture quotations taken from THE HOLY BIBLE, TODAY'S NEW INTERNATIONAL VERSION. Copyright © 2002 by International Bible Society. Used by permission of Hodder & Stoughton Publishers, a member of the Hodder Headline Group. All rights reserved.